Song of Songs

Second Edition

THE PASSION TRANSLATION

Translated from the Hebrew and Aramaic Texts
Dr. Brian Simmons

5 Fold Media
Visit us at www.5foldmedia.com

Published by 5 Fold Media, LLC
www.5foldmedia.com

ISBN: 978-1-936578-59-7
Library of Congress Control Number: 2013934804

Dedication

Dedicated to every passionate lover of Jesus.
May the Holy Spirit take you by the hand
and lead you out in pursuit of your Beloved!

Translator's Introduction

Allow me to explain a few things about *The Passion Translation*. To translate God's Word from Hebrew into another language is both a difficult and delightful task. The Passion Translation has been a project I've wanted to give myself to for many years. And recently, it seemed the Lord spoke deeply into my heart that He wanted me to make this project a reality. So I have begun with my favorite book in the Bible, the Song of Solomon, known as the Song of Songs.

I have fallen in love with this sweetest song of all the ages. Breathtaking and beautiful, we see the Shulamite journey unveiled in this anointed allegory. It is the path every passionate lover will choose. It becomes a journey that not only describes the divine parable penned by Solomon, but a journey that every longing lover of Jesus will find as his or her very own.

So why another translation? Many wonderful versions of our Bible now grace our bookshelves, bookstores, software programs, even applications on our phones. So why add one more? The reason is simple: God wants His message of love to be received in every culture, community, and language. So, what about the language of love? There is a language of the heart that must express the passion of this love-theology. That is the purpose of *The Passion Translation*.

By translating this most holy portion of the Word of God, the Song of Songs, I have attempted to translate not only from a scholarly or linguistic perspective but from the passion of a heart on fire. Love will always find a language to express itself. Fiery love for Jesus pushes our thoughts out of hiding and puts them into anointed words of adoration. This articulation, out of the deepest places of our hearts, moves God and inspires each of us to a greater devotion. Everyone deserves to hear and feel the passion of our Bridegroom for His radiant and soon to be perfected bride.

The inspired Song of Songs is a work of art. It is a melody sung from the heart of Jesus Christ for His longing bride. It is full of symbols, subtle art forms, poetry, and nuances that the translator must convey in order to bring it forth adequately to the English reader. This is what I have attempted to do with this project. Some of the cultural symbols that conveyed rich texture of meaning to the Hebrew speaker nearly three thousand years ago have become almost impossible to leave in its literal form, since the English speaker of today has little or no connection to those symbols. This requires that much of the hidden meanings locked into the Hebrew text be made explicit. This is why I have chosen to make this a dynamic equivalent of transferring the meaning, not just the words, into a form that many will find refreshing.

Moreover, in reading this Shulamite journey, the story line is often missed or overlooked. I believe the Holy Spirit has hidden within the Song of Songs an amazing story—a story of how Jesus makes His bride beautiful and holy by casting out her fear with perfect love! This sent-from-heaven revelation is waiting to be received with all its intensity and power to unlock the deepest places of our hearts!

Unfortunately for some, the Song of Songs has become merely a book expressing sexuality with hidden meanings and symbols of sensuality. Many modern expositors will teach from the Song of Songs the sexual relationship appropriate to a husband and wife. They find it difficult when others see the symbols and apply them to the spiritual journey every believer must take as we move further into the passionate heart of our heavenly Bridegroom. Their fear is that we "over spiritualize" the Song of Songs. How hard this would be! How wonderfully spiritual and holy is this Song of all Songs!

Every symbol the reader encounters must be seen as a form of a "virtual reality" that can, when properly interpreted, help us in our pursuit of Jesus Christ until we are fully His. Truly, if this is the Song of all Songs, its theme goes beyond and reaches higher than mere human sexuality.

So be prepared to see yourself in this journey and to hear His lyrics of love sung over you. Invest the time to simply read this through in one sitting. Then go back through slowly and carefully as you ponder each verse and pray through each love principle revealed in this translation. I think you may be shocked to read some of the things spoken over your life, almost too good to be true! May heaven's glorious Bridegroom, the Beloved of your soul, come and manifest Himself to you in a wonderful and breathtaking fashion as you read *Song of Songs* in *The Passion Translation*! My prayer is that you would be as thrilled with what you read as I have been in translating it!

This book marked the beginning of *The Passion Translation* project, with more books being completed each year. Each book will be faithful to the original language but also true in its expression of the hidden gems within the text. Thank you for your prayers for us and for your support of *The Passion Translation* project.

Overwhelmed by His love,
Brian Simmons

Chapter One

¹The most amazing song of all, by King Solomon

[The Shulamite][a]

²Smother me with kisses—
Your Spirit-kiss divine.[b]
So kind are Your caresses,[c]
I drink them in
Like the sweetest wine![d]
³Your presence releases
A fragrance so pleasing—
Over and over poured out.
For Your lovely name is "Flowing Oil."
No wonder the brides-to-be adore You.
⁴Draw me into Your heart and lead me out,
We will run away together—
Into Your cloud-filled chamber![e]

[The Chorus of Friends]

We will remember Your love

---

a. 1:2 The word for *Shulamite* and the word for *Solomon* are taken from the same Hebrew root word, one masculine, the other feminine. We are one spirit with our King, united with Him. You have become the Shulamite.

b. 1:2 This Spirit-kiss is what made Adam, the man of clay, into a living expression of God. Dust and Deity meet as the Maker kissed His Spirit wind into Adam. The Word of God is the kiss from the mouth of our Beloved, breathing upon us the revelation of His love.

c. 1:2 Or, "Your breasts," or "Your loves." The Hebrew literally means "Your loves." This speaks of His saving love, keeping love, forgiving love, and embracing love. The love of Jesus cannot be singular, it is so infinite it must be described in the plural.

d. 1:4 There is a wordplay in the Hebrew, similar to a pun. The word for "kisses" and the Hebrew word for "take a drink (wine)," is nearly the same. The implication, as seen by ancient expositors, is that God's lovers will be drunk with love, the intoxicating kisses of His mouth. The Hebrew word for kiss is "nashaq," which can also mean "to equip," or "to arm (for battle)." We needs His kisses to become equipped warriors for Him.

e. 1:4 The Hebrew literally means "a chamber inside a chamber." This points us to the Holy of Holies inside the Temple chamber.

As we laugh and rejoice in You,
Celebrating Your every kiss
As better-than-wine.
No wonder righteousness
Adores You!

[The Shulamite]

⁵Jerusalem maidens,
In this twilight darkness[a]
I know I am so unworthy—so in need!

[The Shepherd-King]

Yet you are so lovely!

[The Shulamite]

I feel as dark and dry as the desert tents
Of the wandering nomads![b]

[The Shepherd-King]

Yet you are so lovely—
Like the fine linen tapestry
Hanging in the Holy Place!

[The Shulamite to her friends]

⁶Please don't stare in scorn
Because of my dark and sinful ways.[c]
My angry brothers quarreled with me
And appointed me guardian
Of their ministry-vineyards
Yet I've not guarded
My vineyard-within
⁷Won't You tell me, Lover of my soul
Where do You feed Your flock?

---

a. 1:5 Or "black." The Hebrew root word used here for "black" or "dark" means "twilight darkness" or "morning grey."

b. 1:5 Literally, "dark as the tent curtains of Kedar." There is a wordplay in the Hebrew, as the word *Kedar* means "a dark one," or "a dark place." This was the name of one of the sons of Ishmael and represents our old, Adam-life.

c. 1:6 The Hebrew literally means "Many morning suns have darkened me."

Where do You lead Your beloved ones[a]
To rest in the heat of the day?
For I wish to be wrapped all around you,[b]
As I go among the flocks of Your under-shepherds.
It is You I long for with no veil between us!

[The Shepherd-King]

[8]Listen, My radiant one—
If you ever lose sight of Me
Just follow in My footsteps
Where I lead My lovers.
Come with your burdens and cares.[c]
Come to the place near
The sanctuary of My shepherds—
There you will find Me.
[9]My dearest one,
Let Me tell you how I see you—
You are so thrilling to Me.
To gaze upon you is like looking
At one of Pharaoh's finest horses—
A strong, regal steed
Pulling his royal chariot.
[10]Your tender cheeks are aglow—
Your earrings and gem-laden necklaces
Set them ablaze.
[11]We will enhance your beauty[d]
Encircling you
With Our golden reins of love
You will be marked
With Our redeeming grace.[e]

a. 1:7 She sees her Beloved as a Shepherd. This is a metaphor of the role He takes in her eyes. We need not develop a literal story line of a lover and a shepherd, but you and your Beloved, who cannot be described by one symbol or role.

b. 1:7 Translated from the Septuagint.

c. 1:8 Or, "graze your goats." This is a metaphor that speaks of her responsibilities and labors.

d. 1:11 This is the Trinity ("We") which will be involved in making every Shulamite holy and radiant.

e. 1:11 The Hebrew literally means "inlaid with silver." The concept of silver in the Bible always points to redemption, the price paid to set us free.

[The Shulamite]
¹²As the King surrounded me,
The sweet fragrance of my praise-perfumeᵃ
Awakened the night.
¹³A sachet of myrrh is My Lover,
Like a tied-up-bundle of myrrhᵇ
Resting over my heart.
¹⁴Like a bouquet of Henna blossoms,
I will hold Him and never let Him part—
Henna plucked near the vines
At the fountain of the Lamb.ᶜ

[The Shepherd-King]
¹⁵Look at you, My dearest darling,
You are so lovely!
You are beauty itself to Me.
Your passionate eyes
Are like loyal, gentle doves.ᵈ

[The Shulamite]
¹⁶My Beloved One,
You are pleasing beyond words,
And so winsome!
Our resting place is anointed and flourishing
Like a green forest meadow bathed in light.
¹⁷Rafters of cedar branches are over our heads
And balconies of pleasant smelling pines.
A perfect home!

---

a. 1:12 Or "spikenard."

b. 1:13 This bundle of tied up myrrh is an incredible picture of the cross. Myrrh, known as an embalming spice, is always associated with suffering. The suffering love of Jesus will now be over her heart for the rest of her days—the revelation of our Beloved tied as a bundle onto the cross.

c. 1:14 The Hebrew word for "henna" is a homonym that can mean "atonement" or "redeeming grace." *Engedi* can be translated, "the fountain of the Lamb."

d. 1:15 The Hebrew literally means "your eyes are doves." Some see this as a hypocorism, but the dove points us to the Holy Spirit. She is commended for seeing Him now with spiritual revelation as she perceives the glory of the cross with its "myrrh."

Chapter Two

¹I'm truly His rose,
The very theme of His song!ᵃ
I'm overshadowed by His love,
Growing in the valley!

[The Shepherd-King]
²Yes, you are My darling companion.
You stand out from all the rest,
For though the curse of sin surrounds youᵇ
Still you remain pure as a lily,ᶜ
Even more than all others.

[The Shulamite]
³My Beloved is to me
As the finest, fragrant apple tree—
He stands above the sons of men,ᵈ
Sitting under His grace-shadow,
I blossom in His shade.
Enjoying the sweet taste
Of His pleasant, delicious fruit.
Resting with delight where His glory never fades.
⁴Suddenly, He transported me
Into His house of wine—

---

a. 2:1 The Hebrew text says, "a rose of Sharon." The word *Sharon* can be translated 'his song.' She now sees herself as the one He sings over! The root word for rose (Hebrew: "habab") can mean "overshadowed."

b. 2:2 This is literally a thorn bush, which speaks of the curse of sin. See Genesis 3:18, John 19:5, and Galatians 3:13. On the cross, Jesus wore a crown of thorns for He took away the curse of sin.

c. 2:2 The emblem of a lily was engraved on the upper part of the pillars of Solomon's Temple. Lilies are symbols of purity in the "temple" of our inner being.

d. 2:3 Or, "trees of the forest. Trees in the Bible are often metaphors for humanity.

He looked upon me
With His unrelenting love Divine.[a]
[5]Revive me with Your goblet of wine
Refresh me again with Your sweet promises!
Help me and hold me for I am love-sick![b]
I'm longing for more—
Yet how could I take more?[c]
[6]His left hand cradles my head
While His right hand holds me close.[d]
I'm at rest in this love!

[The Shepherd-King]
[7]**Promise Me, brides-to-be,**
By the gentle gazelles[e]
And delicate deer,
That you'll not disturb My love
Until she is ready to arise.

[The Shulamite]
[8]Listen! I hear my Lover's voice!
I know it's Him coming to me—
Leaping with joy over mountains.
Skipping in love
Over the hills that separate us,[f]
To come to me.
[9]Let me describe Him:
He is graceful as a gazelle—
Swift as a wild stag
Now He comes closer,
Even to the places where I hide.

---

a. 2:4 Or, "His banner covering me was love."

b. 2:5 Or, "wounded by love."

c. 2:5 Implied in the context.

d. 2:6 For more on the right hand and left hand see Proverbs 3:16.

e. 2:7 In the poetic imagery of the Song of Songs, deer and gazelle become symbols of the joys of love. The Septuagint is, "by all the powers and strengths of the field."

f. 2:8 Implied in the context of 2:17.

Now He gazes into my soul,
Peering through the portal
As He blossoms within my heart.
¹⁰The One that I love calls to me:

[The Bridegroom-King]
Arise, My dearest!
Hurry, My darling,
Come along with Me!
I have come as you have asked
To draw you to my heart and lead you out!
For now is the time My beautiful one.
¹¹The season has now changed,
The bondage of your
Barren winter has ended
And the season of hiding is over and gone.
The rains have soaked the earth,ᵃ
¹²And left it bright
With blossoming flowers.
The season for pruning the vines
Has arrived.ᵇ
I hear the cooing of doves in our landᶜ
Filling the air with songs
To awaken you and guide you forth.
¹³Can you not discern
This new day of destiny
Breaking forth around you?
The early signs of My purposes and plans
Are bursting forth.ᵈ
The budding vines of new life

---

a. 2:11 The rains speak of the outpouring of the Holy Spirit. She is refreshed and prepared to move out with Him.

b. 2:12 Or, "the season of singing." The Hebrew words for "singing" and "pruning" are virtually identical.

c. 2:12 This is the turtle-dove which is heard only at the time of harvest. The turtle-dove is also an acceptable sacrifice of cleansing in the place of a lamb. The words, our land, shows the joint-possession of all things that we enjoy through our union with Christ.

d. 2:13 This is literally "the fig tree has sweetened and puts forth its early figs." In the language of allegory, the fig tree becomes a picture of destiny and purpose. The sign of a fig tree blooming is the sign of an early spring, a new season.

Are now blooming everywhere;
The fragrance of their flowers whispers:
"There is change in the air."
Arise My love, My beautiful companion
And run with Me to the higher place.
For now is the time to arise
And come away with Me!
[14]For you are My dove,
Hidden in the split open Rock.[a]
It was I who took you
And hid you up high
In the secret stairway of the sky.
Let Me see your radiant face
And hear your sweet voice.[b]
How beautiful your eyes of worship,
And I love the sound
Of your voice in prayer.
[15]You must catch the troubling foxes,
Those sly little foxes
Which hinder our relationship.[c]
For they raid
Our budding vineyard of love
To ruin what I've planted within you.
Will you catch them
And remove them for Me?
We will do it together.

[The Shulamite]

[16]I know my Lover is mine
And I have everything in You

---

a. 2:14 This speaks of the wounded side of Jesus, our Rock where we hide and rest.

b. 2:14 The Hebrew literally means "your voice is delicious."

c. 2:15 These "foxes" are the compromises that have hidden deep in our hearts. These are areas of our lives where we have not yet allowed the victory of Christ to shine into. The foxes keep the fruit of His Spirit from growing within us.

For we delight ourselves in each other.[a]
[17]But, until the day springs to life
And the shifting shadows of fear disappear,
Turn around, my Lover, and ascend
To the holy mountains of separation
Without me.[b]
Until the new day fully dawns,
Run on ahead like the graceful gazelle
And skip like the young stag
Over the mountains of separation.
Go on ahead to the mountain of spices—
I'll come away another time.[c]

---

a. 2:16 The Hebrew includes the phrase, "He browses among the lilies." The Hebrew word for browse can also mean "to take delight in."

b. 2:17 This literally means "mountains of Bether," the Hebrew word for separation or gap. This could be the realm of holiness, being separated to God. Some scholars say Bether was a spiritual representation of a mountain of fragrant spices—i.e., the realm of holiness.

c. 2:17 Implied in the text.

Chapter Three

¹Night after night I'm tossing and turning
On my bed of travail.
Why did I let Him go from me?
How my heart now aches for Him
But He is nowhere to be found!
²So I must rise in search of Him,
Looking throughout the city,[a]
Seeking until I find Him.
Even if I have to roam through every street,
Nothing will keep me from my search.
Where is He—my soul's true love?
Nowhere to be found!
³Then I encountered the overseers
As they circled the city.
So I asked them:
"Have you found Him—
My heart's true Love?"
⁴Just as I moved past them
I encountered Him,
I found the One I adore!
I caught Him and fastened myself to Him,
Refusing to be feeble in my heart again.
Now I'll bring Him back to the temple within
Where I was given new birth—
Into my innermost parts,
The place of my conceiving.

---

a. 3:2 The city is a picture of the local church, a place with government, order, and overseers. She goes from church to church looking for the One she loves.

[The Bridegroom-King]
>⁵Promise Me, O Jerusalem maidens,
By the gentle gazelles and delicate deer,
That you'll not disturb My love
Until she is ready to arise.

[The Voice of the Lord]
>⁶Who is this One
Ascending from the wilderness
In the pillar of the glory cloud?
He is fragrant with the anointing oils
Of myrrh and frankincense—ᵃ
More fragrant than all the spices of the merchant.
⁷Look! It is the King's marriage-carriage!
The love-seat surrounded by sixty champions—
The mightiest of Israel's host
Like pillars of protection.
⁸They are angelic warriors standing ready
With swords to defend the King and His fiancé
From every terror of the night
⁹The King made this mercy seat for Himself
Out of the finest wood that will not decay.
¹⁰Pillars of smoke, like silver mist—
A canopy of golden glory dwells above it.
The place where they sit together
Is sprinkled with crimson.
Love and mercy cover this carriage,
Blanketing His tabernacle-throne.
The King Himself has made it
For those who will become His bride!
¹¹Rise up Zion maidens, brides-to-be!
Come and feast your eyes on this King
As He passes in procession
On His way to His wedding!

---

a. 3:6 These spices are found in the Bible as ingredients of the sacred anointing oil. Myrrh points to the sufferings and death of Christ while frankincense reveals the fragrance of His perfect life and ministry.

This is the day filled
With overwhelming joy—
The day of His great gladness!

Chapter Four

[The Bridegroom-King]
¹Listen, My dearest darling,
You are so beautiful—
You are beauty itself to Me!
Your eyes glisten with love,
Like gentle doves behind your veil.
What devotion I see
Each time I gaze upon you.
You appear to Me
Like a sacrifice ready to be offered.[a]
²When I look at you I see
How you have taken My fruit
And tasted My Word.
Your life has become clean and pure,
Like sheep washed and newly shorn.
You now show grace and balance
With truth on display.
³Your lips are lovely
As Rahab's scarlet ribbon,[b]
Speaking mercy, speaking grace!
The words of your mouth
Are refreshing as an oasis.
What pleasure you bring to Me!

a. 4:1 The Hebrew literally means "your hair is like a flock of goats streaming down Mount Gilead." There is great symbolism in this verse. Hair is a symbol of our devotion to Christ. Mount Gilead is where the sacrificial animals were kept in preparation of Temple sacrifice, and a goat coming down Mount Gilead was a sacrifice ready to be offered.

b. 4:3 This "scarlet ribbon" in the text is an obvious comparison to the scarlet ribbon Rahab placed at her dwelling to show the place where mercy would spare her life. The color scarlet points us to the blood of mercy, Christ's sacrifice that has spared us. See Joshua 2.

I see your blushing cheeks
Opened like the halves of a pomegranate[a]
Showing through your veil
Of tender meekness.
How passionate your personality!
[4]When I look at you
I see your inner strength,
So stately and strong.
You are as secure as David's fortress.
Your virtues and grace
Cause a thousand famous soldiers
To surrender to your beauty.
[5]Your pure faith and love
Rest over your heart
As you nurture those
Who are yet infants!

[The Shulamite]

[6]I've made up my mind.
Until the darkness disappears
And the dawn has fully come,
In spite of shadows and fears—
I will go to the mountain top with You.
I will climb with You
The mountain of suffering love[b]
And the hill of burning incense.
Yes, I will be Your bride.

[The Bridegroom King]

[7]Every part of you
Is so beautiful, My darling!
Perfect your beauty,
Without flaw within!

a. 4:3 Pomegranates were engraved on the top of the pillars of Solomon's Temple and were also sewn into the hem of the robe of the High Priest. They speak of our opened hearts of love, filled with passion for Him.

b. 4:6 Literally, "the Mountain of myrrh"–the emblem of suffering love. To become the bride, she must experience Calvary, as did her Lord. We must be His co-crucified partner that will embrace the fellowship of His sufferings. See Galatians 2:20, Philippians 3:10.

⁸Now you are ready, bride of the mountains,
To come with Me as we climb
The highest peaks together.
Come with Me through the archway of trust,ᵃ
We will look down
From the crest of the glistening mounts
And from the summit
Of our sublime sanctuary.
Together we will wage war
In the lion's den and the leopard's lair
As they watch nightly for their prey.
⁹For you reach into My heart.
With one flash of your eyes
I am undone by your love,
My beloved one, My equal, My bride.
You leave me breathless—
I am overcome
By merely a glance
From your worshipping eyes
And you have stolen My heart.
I'm held hostage by your love
And by the graces of
Righteousness upon you!ᵇ
¹⁰How satisfying to Me,
My equal, My bride.
Your love is My finest wine,
Intoxicating and thrilling—
And your sweet praise-perfume
So exotic, so pleasing.
¹¹Your loving words
Are like honey to Me,
Drenched with worship.
Your tongue releases milk and honey,

a. 4:8 Translated from the Septuagint.
b. 4:9 Literally, "the ornaments of your neck."

For I find the Promised Land
Flowing within you.
The fragrance of your worshipping love
Surrounds you with
Scented robes of white.
¹²My darling bride,
My private paradise
Fastened to My heart.
A secret spring are you
That no one else can have—
My bubbling fountain
Hidden from public view.
What a perfect partner to Me,
Now that I have you!
¹³⁻¹⁴Your inward life is now sprouting,
Bringing forth fruit.
What a beautiful paradise
Unfolds within you!
When I'm near you
I smell aromas of the finest spice
I find many clusters
Of My exquisite fruit growing within
Your inner garden—
Here are nine:
Pomegranates of passion,[a]
Henna from heaven,[b]
Spikenard so sweet,[c]
Saffron shining,[d]
Fragrant calamus from the cross,[e]

---

a. 4:13-14 *Pomegranate* is taken from a word that means "exalted"—the temple pillars were adorned with pomegranates.

b. 4:13-14 *Henna* comes from a root word for "ransom price" or redemption. The fruit of mercy is seen in His maturing bride.

c. 4:13-14 The Hebrew root word for *spikenard* is "light." She is walking in the light as He is in the Light.

d. 4:13-14 Saffron is the crocus, the lover's perfume, costly and fragrant.

e. 4:13-14 Calamus is taken from a marsh plant known as "sweet flag," that produces fragrant oil. The Hebrew word for this spice means "purchased" or "redeemed."

Sacred cinnamon,[a]
Branches of scented woods,[b]
Myrrh, like tears from a tree,[c]
And aloes as eagles ascending.[d]
[15]Your life flows into Mine
Pure as a garden spring—
A well of living water
Springs up from within you.
You are like a mountain brook
Flowing into My heart!

[The Shulamite Bride]

[4:16-5:1]Then may Your awakening breath
Blow upon my life until I am fully Yours.
Breathe upon me with Your Spirit-winds.
Stir up the sweet spice of Your life within me.
Spare nothing as You make me
Your fruit-filled garden,
Hold nothing back
Until I release Your fragrance.
Come walk with me as You walked
With Adam in Your paradise-garden.[e]
Come taste the very fruits of Your life in me.

[The Bridegroom King]

I have come to you,
My bride, My darling
For you are My paradise-garden!

---

a. 4:13-14 Cinnamon emits a fragrance that is representative of an odor of holiness to the Lord. This was used in the sacred anointing oil of the priests and tabernacle.

b. 4:13-14 This is the incense that would be burned on the golden altar in the Holy Place.

c. 4:13-14 Known as "tears from a tree," myrrh was a resin-spice formed by cutting a tree. It is an obvious picture of the suffering love of Christ dripping down from Calvary's tree.

d. 4:13-14 Aloes are considered by many as the healing balm. The presence of the Lord within her is now released as healing balm to those she touches. Jesus' robes smelled of aloes (Psalm 45:8). One of the names used by some for aloes is the "Eagle Wood." Like eagles, we fly above our wounds, free from the past as we walk in intimacy with Him.

e. 4:16-5:1 The scene of a garden and the breath of God point us back to the Paradise of Eden. Now this paradise is found in His bride. This is the reason why the reference of Adam is given, to help the reader connect with the mystery of this scene.

[The Shulamite Bride]

Come walk into me
Until I am fully Yours
Come taste the fruits
Of Your life in me.

Chapter Five

[The Bridegroom King]
I have gathered from your heart,
My equal, My bride,
I have gathered from My garden
All My sacred spices—even My myrrh!
I have tasted and enjoyed
My wine within you.
I have tasted with pleasure
My pure milk, My honeycomb
Which you yield to Me.
I delight in gathering My sacred spice,
All the fruits of My life
I have gathered from within you,
My paradise-garden!
Come all My friends—
Feast upon My bride!
All you revelers of My palace—
Now feast on her, My lovers!
Drink and drink, and drink again
Until you can take no more—
Drink the wine of her love.
Take all you desire, you priests!
My life within her
Will now become your feast![a]

---

a. 4:16-5:1 The beautiful bride overflowing with His life is now to be given away to others, even as Jesus was given away to us by the Father. She has become a feast for the nations, wine to cheer the hearts of others.

[The Shulamite Bride]
> ²After this I let my devotion slumber,
> But my heart for Him stayed awake.
> I had a dream.
> I dreamed of my Beloved—
> He was coming to me in the darkness of night.
> The melody of the Man I love awakened me.
> I heard His knock at my heart's door
> As He pleaded with me:

[The Bridegroom King]
> "Arise My love,
> Open your heart My darling—
> Deeper still to Me!
> Will you receive Me this dark night?
> There is no one else but you,
> My friend, My equal.
> I need you this night
> To arise and be with Me.
> You are My pure and loyal dove,
> A perfect partner for Me.
> My flawless one, will you arise?
> For My heaviness and tears
> Are more than I can bear.
> I have spent Myself for you
> Throughout the dark night."[a]

[The Sleeping Bride]
> ³"I have already laid aside
> My own garments for You.
> How could I take them up again

---

a. 5:2 The Hebrew text literally means "My head is filled with dew and My hair with the drops of the night." This is clearly a picture of Jesus as the Gethsemane Man, the One who prayed all night for us (John 17). The translation takes the liberty of taking the implicit and making it explicit in order to express the dynamic equivalent and aid the reader in understanding the scene.

Since I've yielded my righteousness to Yours?[a]
You have cleansed my life and taken me so far,
Isn't that enough?"
[4]My Beloved reached into me
To unlock my heart—
The core of my very being
Trembled at His touch.
How my soul melted when He spoke to me!
[5]My spirit arose to open
For more of His touch,
As I surrendered to Him
I began to sense His fragrance;
The fragrance of His suffering love!
It was the scent of myrrh
Flowing all through me!
[6]I opened my soul to my Beloved,
But so suddenly He was gone!
And my heart was torn out
In longing for Him!
I sought His closeness, His fragrance—
But could not find Him anywhere.
I called out for Him—
Yet He did not answer me.
I will arise and search for Him
Until I find Him!
[7]As I walked throughout the city
In search of Him
The overseers happened to find me
As they made their rounds.
They beat me and bruised me
Until I could take no more.
In my wounding they removed
Their "covering" from me,

---

a. 5:3 Garments in the Bible are frequently used as a picture of righteousness. Filthy garments are a symbol of unrighteousness or self-righteousness. Clean and white garments are a picture of the righteousness of Christ. Laying aside "her garments" is a symbolic picture of what happens once we come to know Jesus as Savior—we lay aside our self-righteousness and take up His garments.

⁸Nevertheless, make me this promise,
You brides-to-be,
If you find my Beloved One
Please tell Him
I endured all travails for love of Him.
I've been pierced through by love,ᵃ
And I will not be turned aside!

[Jerusalem maidens, brides-to-be]
⁹*What love is this?*
How could you continue to care
So deeply for Him?
Isn't there another that could
Steal away your heart?
We see now your beauty,
More beautiful than all the others.
What makes your Beloved
Better than another?
What is it about Him
That makes you ask
That we promise you so?

[The Shulamite Bride]
¹⁰He alone is my Beloved.
He shines in dazzling splendor,
Yet still so approachable.
Without equal as He stands above all others—
Waving His banner to myriads!
¹¹The way He leads me is divine.
His leadership—so pure and dignified
As He wears His crown of gold.
Upon this crown are letters of black

---

a. 5:8 As translated from the Septuagint.

Written on a background of glory.[a]
¹²He sees everything with pure understanding.
How beautiful His insights—without distortion.
His eyes rest upon the fullness
Of the river of revelation
Flowing so clean and pure!
¹³Looking at His gentle face
I see such fullness of emotion.
Like a lovely garden where fragrant spices grow—[b]
What a Man!
No one speaks words so anointed as this One—[c]
Words that both pierce and heal,
Words like lilies dripping with myrrh.
¹⁴See how His hands hold unlimited power!
But He never uses it in anger,
For He is always holy, displaying His glory.
His innermost place is a work of art—
So beautiful and bright.
How magnificent and noble is this One—
Covered in majesty!
¹⁵He's steadfast in all He does,
Never veering.
His ways are the ways
Of righteousness,
Based on truth and holiness.
None can rival Him,
But all will be amazed by Him!
¹⁶Most sweet are His kisses,
Even His whispers of love.
He is delightful in every way

a. 5:11 Many Jewish interpreters have seen the phrase, "His locks are black as a raven" as pointing us to the letters of the Law written in heaven. Jewish rabbis teach that the precepts of the Word of God (Torah) are written in the heavenly realm, with black letters on top of white flames of glory fire. (Hebrew letters can appear as the locks of hair.)

b. 5:13 The Hebrew literally means "like a tower of fragrance." These beds of spices would picture a garden of emotion and sweetness coming forth from her Beloved.

c. 5: 13 See Psalm 45:2, a Psalm with an inscription stating it was written to the "tune of lilies."

And perfect from every viewpoint.
If you ask me why I love Him so,
O brides-to-be,
It is because there is none like Him to me.
Everything about Him
Fills me with holy desire!
And now He is my Beloved—
My forever Friend!

Chapter Six

[Brides-to-be]

¹*O rarest of beauty,*
Where then has your Lover gone?
We long to see Him too!
Where may we find Him?
As you seek after Him
We will follow you.

[The Shulamite Bride]

²My Lover has gone down
Into His garden of delight,
The place where His spices grow
To feast with those pure in heart.
I know we shall find Him there.
³He is within me—I am His garden of delight.
I have Him fully and now He fully has me!

[The Bridegroom-King]

⁴O My beloved, you are striking—
Lovely even in your weakness!
When I see you in your beauty
I see a radiant city,
Where we will dwell as one.^a
More pleasing than any pleasure,
More delightful than any delight.
You have ravished My heart,

a. 6:4 The text includes a reference to Jerusalem. For the Jew, it is the city where God and man lived together. For the believer, it points us to the New Jerusalem, where God and man dwell in holy union.

Stealing away My strength to resist you,
Even hosts of angels stand in awe of you![a]
[5]Turn your eyes from Me,
I can't take it anymore!
I can't resist the passion
Of the eyes that I adore.
Overpowered by a glance,
My ravished heart—undone,
Held captive by your love
I'm truly overcome![b]
For your undying devotion to Me
Is the most yielded sacrifice.[c]
[6]The shining of your spirit[d]
Shows how you have taken My truth
And become balanced and complete!
[7]Your beautiful blushing cheeks
Reveal how real your passion is for Me,
Even hidden behind a veil of humility.
[8]I could have chosen any from among
The vast multitude of the royal ones
Who follow Me.[e]
[9]But one is My beloved dove—
Unrivaled in your beauty,
Without equal, beyond compare,
The perfect one, the only one for Me.
Others see your beauty and sing of your joy,
Brides and queens chant her praise:
"How blessed is she!"

---

a. 6:4 This is how various Hebrew scholars have interpreted the phrase: "you have captured my heart," or "awe inspiring as an army with banners."

b. 6:5 The Hebrew word for "overcome" is the word, Rahab. Like the harlot Rahab who was chosen, favored, saved from Jericho's destruction, and included into the genealogy of Jesus, so you have "rahab-ed" His heart. No one would have thought that Rahab would be the one to be honored, and many have said that about you. You have overcome many things, but to overcome Him is love's delight.

c. 6:5 Literally, "Your hair is like a wave of goats streaming down Mount Gilead." We see the hair as a picture of our devotion to Christ. See also Song of Songs 4:1.

d. 6:6 The word used in most translations is *teeth*, which is taken from a Hebrew root word which some believe means "white" or "shining." With our teeth we chew the Word of God and process its truth.

e. 6:8 The Hebrew literally means "sixty queens, eighty brides, and endless numbers of women."

¹⁰Look at you now—
Arising as the dayspring of the dawn,
Fair as the shining moon.
Bright and brilliant
As the sun in all its strength.
Astonishing to behold
As a majestic army
Waving banners of victory!

[The Shulamite Bride]
¹¹I decided to go down to the valley streams
Where the orchards of the King grow and mature.
I longed to know if hearts were opening
Are the budding vines blooming with new growth—
Has their springtime
Of passionate love yet arrived?
¹²Suddenly my longings transported me!
My divine desire brought me
Next to My Beloved Prince,
Sitting with Him in His royal chariot.
We were lifted up together!ᵃ

[Zion maidens, Brides-to-be]
¹³Come back! Return to us, O maiden of His majesty,
Dance for us as we gaze upon your beauty!

[The Shulamite Bride]
Why would you seek a mere Shulamite like me?
Why would you want to see my dance of love?

[The Bridegroom-King]
Because you dance so gracefully
As though you danced with angels!ᵇ

---

a. 6:12 Considered to be the most difficult verse to translate in the Song of Songs, the meaning of the Hebrew is uncertain.

b. 6:13 This is literally the "dance of Mahanaim" or "the dance of two armies." When Jacob (Israel) returned to the Promised Land, he entered at Mahanaim, the place where two camps of angels gathered. See Genesis 32:1-2.

Chapter Seven

¹How beautiful on the mountains
Are the sandaled feet of this one
Bringing such good news.
You are truly royalty!
How you walk so gracefully in My ways
Displays such dignity.
You are truly the poetry of God—
His very handiwork!
²⁻³Out of your innermost being
Is flowing the fullness of My Spirit—
Never failing to satisfy.
Within your womb there is
A birthing of harvest-wheat;
They are the sons and daughters
Who will be nurtured
By the purity you impart.
How gracious you have become!
⁴Your life now stands tall as a tower;
Like a shining light on a hill.
Your revelation-eyes are pure,
As pools of refreshing;
Sparkling light for a multitude!
Such great discernment now surrounds you,
Protecting you from the enemy's advance.
⁵Redeeming love crowns you as royalty.
Your thoughts are full of
Life, wisdom, and virtue.

Even a King is held captive by your beauty!
⁶How delicious your fair beauty
It cannot be described
As I count the delights you bring to Me—
Love has become the greatest!
⁷You stand in victory above the rest,
Stately and secure
As you share with Me
Your vineyard of love.
⁸Now I decree,
I will ascend and arise.
I will take hold of you with My power,
Possessing every part of My fruitful bride.
Your love I will drink as wine,
And your words will be Mine.
⁹For your kisses of love
Are exhilarating
More than any delight
I have known before.
Your kisses of love awaken
Even the lips of sleeping ones
To kiss Me as you have done.

[The Shulamite Bride]
¹⁰Now I know that I am filled with my Beloved
And all His desires are fulfilled in me!
¹¹Come away, my Lover,
Come with me to the far away fields.
We will run away together
To the forgotten places
And show them redeeming love.
¹²Let us arise and run
To the vineyards of Your people
To see if the budding vines of love

Are now in full bloom!
We will see
If their passion is awakened.[a]
There I will display my love for You!
[13]The love-apples are in bloom,
Sending forth their fragrance of spring.
The rarest of fruits are found at our doors
The new as well as the old
I have stored them for You
My Lover-Friend!

---

a. 7:12 Pomegranates are equated to human passion and emotions. When opened, they are a blushing fruit and speak powerfully of our hearts of passion opened to our Lover.

Chapter Eight

[1]If only I could show everyone
This passionate desire I have for You.
If only I could express it fully
No matter who was watching me,
Without shame or embarrassment.
[2]I long to bring you
To my innermost chamber—
This holy sanctuary
You have formed within me.
O, that I might carry You
Completely within me.
I would give You there
The spiced wine of my love
This full cup of bliss which we share.
We would drink our fill until...
[3]His left hand cradles my head
While His right hand holds me close.
We are at rest in this love!
[4]Promise me, brides-to-be,
By the gentle gazelles and delicate deer,
That you'll not disturb my love
Until He is ready to arise.

[The Bridegroom-King]
[5]**Who is this one? Look at her now!**
She arises from her desert of difficulty
Clinging to her Beloved.
When I awakened you

Under the apple tree;
As you were feasting upon Me
I awakened your innermost being
With the travail of birth
As you longed for more of Me.
[6]Fasten Me upon your heart
As a seal of fire forevermore.
This living, consuming flame
Will seal you as My prisoner of love![a]
My love will be stronger than
The chains of death and the grave,
Consuming as the very flashes of fire
From the burning heart of God.
Place this fierce, unrelenting fire
Over all your being!
[7]Rivers of persecution and pain
Will never extinguish this flame.
Endless floods will be unable
To quench this raging fire
Burning within you.
Everything will be consumed,
It will stop at nothing
As you yield everything
To this furious fire—
Until it won't even seem to you
Like a sacrifice anymore!

[The Shulamite Bride]
[8-10]My brothers said to me when I was young:
"Our sister is so immature
What will we do to guard her
For her wedding day?"

---

a. 8:6 The ancient Hebrew word for *seal* can also be translated "prison cell." He longs for His bride to be His love-prisoner, in the prison cell of His eternal love.

[The Bridegroom-King]
"We will build a tower of redemption
To protect her.
Since she is vulnerable
We will enclose her
With a wall of cedar boards."

[The Shulamite Bride]
But now I have grown and become a bride
And my love for Him has made me
A tower of passion and
Contentment for my Beloved
I am now a firm wall of protection for others
Guarding them from harm.
This is how He sees me—
I am the one who brings Him bliss,
Finding favor in His eyes!
[11]My Bridegroom-King has a vineyard of love
Made from a multitude of followers.[a]
His caretakers of this vineyard
Have given my Beloved their best.
[12]But as for my own vineyard of love
I give it all to You forever.
And I will give double honor
To those who serve my Beloved
And have watched over my soul.
[13]My Beloved,
One with me in my garden,
How marvelous
That my friends, the brides-to-be,
Now hear Your voice and song.
Let me now hear it again!

---

a. 8:11 The Hebrew text literally means "Solomon had a vineyard at Baal-Hamon." The king's vineyard is a picture of the church, the called out multitude of those who follow Jesus. Baal-Hamon can be translated "lord of a multitude," "lord of an uproar," or "lord of wealth."

[The Bridegroom and Bride in Divine Duet]

[14]Arise, My darling!
Come quickly my Beloved.
Come and be the graceful gazelle with Me
Come be like a dancing deer with me.
We will dance in the high place of the sky
Yes, on the mountains of fragrant spice!
Forever we shall be
United as One!

About the Translator

Dr. Brian Simmons is known as a passionate lover of God. After a dramatic conversion to Christ, Brian knew that God was calling him to go to the unreached people of the world and present the gospel of God's grace to all who would listen. He and his wife, Candice, and their three children spent nearly eight years in the tropical rain forest of the Darien Province of Panama as a church planter, translator, and consultant. Brian was involved in the Paya-Kuna New Testament translation project. He studied linguistics and Bible translation principles with New Tribes Mission. After their ministry in the jungle, Brian was instrumental in planting a thriving church in New England (U.S.), and now travels full time as a conference speaker and Bible teacher. He has been happily married to Candice for over forty-two years and is known to boast regularly of his children and grandchildren. Brian and Candice may be contacted at: brian@passiontranslation.com

For more information about the translation project and the Journey of the Bride (A Commentary on the Song of Songs) or any of Brian's books please visit www.stairwayministries.org or www.passiontranslation.com.

More from *The Passion Translation*

John: Eternal Love
Retail Price: $14.95

The book of John brings us a heavenly perspective filled with wonderful revelation in every verse. The writings of John are unique. John was a prophet, a seer, a lover of God, an evangelist, an author, an apostle, and a son of thunder. While the other three gospels give us the history of Jesus Christ, the gospel of John introduces us to Jesus as the Lamb of God, the Good Shepherd, the Kind Forgiver, the Tender Healer, the Compassionate Intercessor, and the Great I Am. To read John's gospel is to encounter Jesus.

Proverbs: Wisdom from Above
Retail Price: $14.95

Proverbs: Wisdom from Above is full of incredible Hebrew and Aramaic secrets that will awaken your heart to the Spirit of Wisdom and Revelation! Prepare for a download of heavenly insights into your destiny, your finances, your relationships, and your life in the Spirit. The gift of wisdom from above is given by a generous Father and He is ready to fill your heart with all that you need to succeed in life and reign with Christ.

More from *The Passion Translation*

Letters from Heaven by the Apostle Paul
(Second Edition)
Retail Price: $12.95

Some of the most beautiful and glorious truths of the Bible are found in the letters of the Apostle Paul. Reading through these letters is like having Paul sitting in your living room personally sharing his experience of the power and majesty of God's Word for His people. Be ready to sense the stirring of the Holy Spirit within you as you read *Letters from Heaven by the Apostle Paul*.

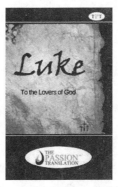

Luke, to the Lovers of God
Retail Price: $10.95

All four Gospels in our New Testament are inspired by God, but Luke's gospel is unique and distinct. It has been described as the loveliest book ever written. Luke writes clearly of the humanity of Jesus—as the servant of all, and the sacrifice for all. In Luke's gospel, every barrier is broken down between Jew and Gentile, men and women, rich and poor. We see Jesus in Luke as the Savior of all who come to Him.

More from *The Passion Translation*

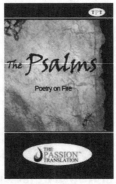

The Psalms, Poetry on Fire
Retail Price: $19.00

The Psalms, Poetry on Fire translated by Dr. Brian Simmons find the words that express our deepest and strongest emotions. The Psalms will turn your sighing into singing and your trouble into triumph. No matter what you may be going through in your life, the Psalms have a message for you! As you read these 150 poetic masterpieces, your heart will be stirred to worship God in greater ways.

"To Establish and Reveal"
For more information visit:
www.5foldmedia.com

Use your mobile device to scan the tag and visit our website. Get the free app: http://gettag.mobi

Like 5 Fold Media on Facebook, follow us on Twitter!